MONST-AGERS

G.J. SMITH

INTRODUCTION

WE SAT IN THE HALF DARK created by the television, quietly watching the final scenes of the movie unfold. Frightened villagers brandished crude weapons and flaming torches, shouting 'Kill the monster!' Cut to the Monster, trudging menacingly forward. Just as the people prepare to attack, they suddenly cower back at the Monster's loud growling, stomping feet and thrashing arms. A classic Frankenstein moment.

Beside me I heard my friend softly say two words. It sounded like "That's rad." Rather high praise for the cinematic moment, I thought. And what 50 year old man uses the word 'rad'? I had to respond.

"That's *rad*?"

A brief pause. We were both still watching the movie. I could hear in his voice that it was his turn to be confused. "Rad? What's rad? And aren't you a little old for that word?"

"You said it first."

"Huh?" There was another brief pause. "Oohh...No. What I said was 'That's Brad'." He pointed at the television. "Brad Peterson"

"Your boss is in this movie?"

"Not exactly, but put a logo polo shirt and khaki pants on that monster and that's Brad."

"Pasty gray complexion?"

"Don't be so literal...Brad doesn't *look* like the monster, but he *acts* like him. He yells and stomps and overreacts to scare and intimidate people. It was the yelling and arm waving that made me recognize him."

I remembered Brad. He had been unexpectedly promoted from another department to manage my friend's team a few weeks ago.

"But the Monster doesn't know how else to act or communicate. He's just trying to survive."

"I suppose. That's probably what Brad is doing too," my friend considered. "The difference is that Brad could *learn* to do better if he really wanted to. I guess being a manager isn't easy, but the effect his behaviors are having on our team is downright frightening."

• • •

He was right. A 'bad' manager can wreak havoc on productivity, morale, creativity and loyalty. This isn't a new concept. There are literally millions of articles, books, seminars and speakers available to help people be more effective and successful leaders. Wonderful wisdom and guidance often supported with valuable data. So why are there still leaders who utilize intimidation, manipulation and micromanagement to manage employees?

There will always be people who thrive on their own importance and power, however I believe the primary offenders do not have ill motives. They are well-intentioned people who are given the job to lead and develop others - Managers, Supervisors, Directors, Executives and Owners - without training, guidance, experience or expectations. Some may have had no intention or desire for the role. They develop strategies out of necessity, survival, often emulating others. Unfortunately, many proceed to erode their work area and teams, not out of malicious intent, but rather due to blindness to their own damaging behaviors. As they remain oblivious, their behaviors trample productivity, suck the life out of morale and make motivation disappear until they are perceived by their team and co-workers with fear and dread. They become monstrous managers or "Monst-agers".

There are two main factors that differentiate a poor manager, a mediocre manager and a great manager - awareness and motivation. To take full advantage of the plethora of great development resources available, Monst-agers need to recognize their own damaging behaviors and be willing to make a change.

USING THIS BOOK

These stories are intended to help managers recognize behaviors and motivate them for change. It's a springboard to the many management resources available. Read it alone or with a group. Use the Discussion Topics section at the end of the book to expand and apply ideas covered in the book.

Something is amiss at the Scaree Costume Company. Vanessa Helsing, new Sr. Manager of Human Resources, witnesses some troubling behaviors and comes face to face with ....Monst-agers.

CHAPTER 1

FRANK STEIN:

BASIC SCARE TACTICS

Vanessa Helsing carried one large box of books and a small box of neatly packed personal items when she moved into the office with the tall windows facing the street. The windows were the first thing she remarked on in the room. The second caused her to let out a brief cry of surprise.

Just behind her mock cherry desk, lurked a strange alien creature. To her left and much closer, a werewolf silently drooled. The red lifeless eyes of a vampire stared at her from the opposite corner. Monsters! Rather than run away, Vanessa laughed. She would be sharing her office with very realistic cutout replicas of a Dracula, the Werewolf and an as yet unidentified space resident. They were just a few of many displayed with pride throughout the Scaree Costume Company where she was, according to the sign on the door, "Senior

Manager of Human Resources"…not that there was a Junior Manager, of course.

She had barely begun unpacking when the company's owner, Mrs. Vera Scaree paid an unexpected visit. After the welcoming small talk, Mrs. Scaree had more to discuss with Vanessa. "This company had been successful for almost 40 years", she began proudly, "building our niche in highly sophisticated costumes for special events, even some television and movies. It requires a blend of artistry, technology and business, bringing together a dynamic blend of talents. Recently, however, the employee enthusiasm, creativity and motivation, which had been the cornerstone of our success, are noticeably absent." Mrs. Scaree had told Vanessa solemnly that she had become especially concerned when there was none of the usual buzz and friendly competition for the upcoming annual costume ball. "You are the new 'people person," she said finally. "Scaree Costumes used to be a fun place and I want that back." Vanessa agreed to begin investigating that very day. It turned out to be easier than she expected.

It began as the result of a near head-on collision in the corridor outside of Conference Room Wand, named for the pictures of Scaree's costumes featuring fairies, wizards and witches that lined the walls. Normally a bright and airy room, its' aura was shattered as a man stormed out, arms waving, voice raised in unintelligible ranting. Vanessa stopped short and barely avoided getting caught in his personal maelstrom. He was oblivious to her presence…or anyone else's it seemed. He continued his noisy, flailing exit down the hallway, unwary employees scampering out of his way. Momentarily stunned, Vanessa remained rooted in her tracks outside the door until he vanished around a corner.

What could have caused that? The man certainly looked like he was under a spell! Fully expecting more frenzied evacuations, Vanessa turned back to the doorway. When nothing happened, she peered cautiously in. She was fascinated to see several other people studiously gathering their belongings, preparing to return to their work areas. No one seemed alarmed. They didn't seem shocked as they left the room, walking slowly past her. She was sure she hadn't imagined that scene!

Intrigued, Vanessa milled around to learn more about this team. She was naturally curious and had found that to be a valuable quality in the HR business. As the people quietly gathered their papers, Vanessa mentally recorded two eye-rolls, one sigh of resignation, some muttering and two people fervently analyzing the carpet on the way out. She almost clapped her hands in delight when she saw Penny Ford leaving the room, juggling folders and her laptop. Vanessa had met Penny during her interview process and moved quickly forward to help her.

"Hello, Penny. How nice to see you again!" Vanessa reached out for the folders in Penny's arms. "It looks like you could use some help."

"Vanessa!" Penny's face brightened, a warm smile appeared. "How nice to see you...and not just because I need a hand. Welcome!"

They shared small talk as they walked. Once in Penny's office, Vanessa broached the topic. "I was in the hall when your meeting ....uh...well, it seemed like your meeting ended rather ...abruptly."

At first Penny looked puzzled. Then she seemed to understand. "Oh. You mean Frank. I'm getting used to it. We all are, I guess."

"Really?" Used to it?? Now she really was interested. "Who is Frank?"

"That's Mr. Stein. Frank Stein. Head of Manufacturing and Distribution," Penny replied with a resigned sigh. "We're a little behind on delivery and he found out that part of the line is down."

"Is it that bad?"

Penny lowered her voice when she answered. "Frank was an OK guy when he worked on the line, but since he became a manager, his standard reaction is over-reaction. He thinks that being loud and intimidating is what makes things happen." With a raised brow and a shrug, Penny expressed her opinion on this theory. The subject changed and they chatted a few more minutes, made plans to meet for lunch the following week and Vanessa headed back to her office.

But the conversation stuck in her head throughout the day. If it was true that the outburst was typical of Frank Stein's managerial style, she was concerned about him as well as the people on the team. It was her job to learn more about the company anyway, so she decided to start with the Manufacturing and Distribution Department the next day.

Using the directory near the elevator to get her bearings, Vanessa arrived in the bustling Manufacturing and Distribution Department about midmorning. She was encouraged by the enthusiastic greeting she received from the first person she encountered, a young woman who introduced herself as Macon Scaree, Summer Intern. (It was a family business, after all.) "Wow! You're just here to learn more about what we do? That's cool! Everybody's gonna want to talk to you." A perplexed frown replaced the smile, . "I guess the first person you want to talk to is the Manager, Mr. Stein."

"If he's not too busy," Vanessa offered.

Macon bit her lip as she thought. "We've got a production line down, so he's not in the best mood…"

"I can imagine he would be frustrated when that happens." Vanessa sympathized.

"Frustrated?" Macon replied with a chuckle. "Try 'going ballistic'." She seemed to catch herself and continued quickly, "Don't get me wrong, he's a good guy and all…let's just go see if he's in his office."

Vanessa followed Macon through a maze of cubicles to a row of offices. As they drew closer to the last office, three people exited, propelled by a tirade of barely intelligible words. She did make out a few…"no excuses", "what were you thinking" and "or else"… the energy was palpable. With a sheepish grin, Macon said, "Oh, good. He's in." They paused outside the door until it was quiet; Macon knocked on the open door, motioned for Vanessa to follow and entered in one move.

Macon announced and introduced Vanessa, offered a quick goodbye and left. Unsure what to expect, Vanessa shouldn't have been surprised by the virtual non-greeting she received from Frank Stein. He stood up for the introduction, said "Hello," then seemed at a loss for words. He was a tall, broad-shouldered man, which she hadn't noticed before. His face showed no emotion. She wondered if he was aware that, without trying, he could look quite imposing.

"Thank you so much for taking the time to see me, Mr. Stein," she began. "I'm excited to join Scaree and want to learn all aspects of the business."

"It's Frank," he said as he sat down, "and I'm not a good teacher. Did I know you were coming?"

Vanessa pressed on. "No. And I certainly don't expect you to teach me. I hope to be spending time in all the departments and just dropped in to introduce myself."

"Oh." He looked at her for a moment, then at his desk, obviously unsure how to proceed.

"I apologize for not calling ahead. I'm visiting all the departments and I just didn't want anyone to be concerned about an 'unidentified woman' lurking around trying to find out the secret to your success." She added a small chuckle to indicate her attempt at humor.

Frank missed it. "I make sure they get things done. Done right. Done on time. There's no secret there!"

That wasn't a good sign...I? They? "Well," she began in her folksiest tone, "even though I don't know much about manufacturing processes, I understand that meeting deadlines with a quality product is important."

"That makes you smarter than some of my employees." Vanessa inwardly winced at the gruff response. Frank continued, "Why should I have to keep after people every day to make sure it happens?"

The look on his face told Vanessa this was not a rhetorical question...he was waiting for an answer. "It is a big job to provide ongoing coaching and motivation to a team."

Frank shook his head. "People know how to do their jobs. Why should I have to reward people for doing their jobs? As my drill sergeant used to say, 'The only motivator they need is my boot.'" Without missing a beat, he stood up and continued, "I'll be glad to give you a short tour of our department."

Vanessa was sure her face must have displayed her shock, but Frank didn't seem to register it. He led Vanessa on an energetic tour of Scaree's manufacturing and distribution systems. He definitely knew his stuff and was committed to the company as well as his team's success. Frank introduced her to several employees with the same warmth one would use to identify plants on a garden tour. Some of the people he had worked with for years prior to his promotion. Every interaction contained an element of criticism or correction. "This is Ellen. She has been here almost 10 years and is the lead on this line. One would expect this to be the best producing line we have." Ellen just smiled uncomfortably.

Frank described the intricate manufacturing systems with an enthusiasm and pride that disappeared when talking with people. Vanessa could sense the tension increase as Frank moved through the maze of machinery. Rather than saying, "Hello", he opened conversations with, "Hey! Why is that conveyor belt running so slow?" or "Do I have to do this myself?" Each time she tried to engage an employee in conversation, Frank declared it was time to move on. A small group of laughing employees looked startled and scattered as Frank approached. Vanessa was a true proponent of Management by Walking Around, but this felt more like Stomping Around, leaving a trampled and flat trail behind. She couldn't tell if he didn't notice or didn't care.

As they waited for the elevator, Vanessa was thinking of how she could possibly talk to Frank about his management style when she was surprised again. Frank turned to her quite earnestly and said, "Maybe you can help me. They seem to like you." She brightened. Perhaps she had read him all wrong. "Before I was promoted, we hardly ever made our goals. When I first took this manager position, we became one of the top performing divisions. Everybody was excited about that. Now, they're starting to slack off again." Vanessa felt her hopes deflating. "It seems like they're only doing the bare minimums to get by and don't seem to care about doing a good job. Will you help me whip them back into shape?"

Vanessa could only look at Frank, speechless. Frank took the brief silence for a yes. "Good. I'll call you later this week." She turned her head towards the 'ding' announcing the elevator. When she turned back, he was gone. "Good-bye." she said quietly to herself.

The time with him was like weight on her shoulders. She practically trudged back to her office. If she felt this way in such a short time, she wondered how his team functioned at all. He was convinced his way - using fear, intimidation, threats and punishment - was right. He believed he was leading his team, and the initial improvements experienced supported his theory. However, since that type of motivation doesn't hold up over time, he was already seeing decreased results.

Vanessa felt that her role as Manager of Human Relations included helping leaders lead. It was possible that Frank did have respect for his crew and their work; however she was pretty sure they didn't feel it. She continued to puzzle on the issue in the back of her mind all day without a resolution. It was going to take much more than a good coaching session to get Frank's attention. She would find out the next day that she wasn't the only one thinking about Frank.

~~~~~~~~~

The department's administrative assistant was on lunch break. Vanessa sat at her desk with the office door open when she heard a quiet knock. Looking up, Vanessa saw a woman peering around the doorframe, who was definitely reading her face, looking for the reaction to the knock...annoyed, curious, warm? Vanessa smiled, recognizing it was Ellen, one of the employees she'd met yesterday in the Manufacturing and Distribution Dept. "Hello, there! It's Ellen, isn't it? Please come in!"

The woman visibly relaxed and returned Vanessa's smile. "Thank you. Yes, I'm Ellen Fielding. We met briefly yesterday."

"Yes," Vanessa nodded. "I'm glad to see you. I hoped to get the opportunity to talk to you about your experiences here at Scaree over the years. I've only been here a few days, so your dedication to the company for 10 years tells me it's a good place to be."

Ellen looked embarrassed, but pleased. "It is a great place to be." She paused. "At least it has been....." Her voice trailed off. Unspoken words hung in the air for a moment, then disappeared. "Frank asked me to bring you this." Ellen handed Vanessa a company mail envelope. "It's a shortcut. Company mail normally gets routed through warehouse in Schenectady," she chuckled. "Even within our office."

"Good to know," Vanessa laughed as she took the envelope, placed it on the desk and returned her attention to Ellen. "I'm so glad you came by. Will you sit down?" Vanessa motioned her to a chair in front of her desk. Ellen looked surprised when Vanessa, rather than move back behind the desk, took the chair next to her. "Tell me a little about yourself."

Ellen seemed to relax as she talked about her family and then about her 'second family' - her co-workers at Scaree. She liked her job and was proud of the fact that she had worked side by side with - and even trained - many people who later moved up in the company. "I trained Frank on some of the machinery when he first came on. That was back when he was Quiet Frank.", she added with a small smile.

Vanessa asked the question with the expression on her face.

"Yup. Quiet Frank. He hardly talked, but he was a good guy and great worker." Her tone turned sad, "Then one day, there was some... "reorganization" they called it and ..poof...Frank's a manager. I think he got chosen because he'd been in the manufacturing business all his life. Plus I don't think anyone else would have said "yes." Then it was like Quiet Frank went home and Manager Frank came in the next day."

"What do you mean? How was he different?"

"Well, first of all, he started strictly enforcing all the rules and even making new ones. Now most of us had complained about the old boss not enforcing some rules and not others, and there's no doubt Frank wanted to make the department better, but...we hadn't had much in the way of 'management' for awhile, so some people liked that things were changing ...and others didn't." Ellen shook her head slightly, "Frank coulda eased in a little more, if you want my opinion!"

Vanessa nodded. She did want Ellen's opinion.

"Of course, he knew our team could be successful, and we were for awhile. But now it seems like no matter what we do, there's something to get on us about. His way is to shout and carry on when things don't go well. *And* when things do go well, he still carries on, cause maybe they *coulda* gone wrong or gone better... who knows??!!" Ellen's voice and exaggerated shrug expressed her frustration. Her final words on the subject stuck with Vanessa for the rest of the day. "I know he thinks he's motivating people...and he's right, in a way. There are a few people in our department who have been motivated to put their resumes out."

Later, when she had a moment, Vanessa opened the envelope Frank had sent. It contained manufacturing data, discipline documentation and a hand scrawled note, "I will call you tomorrow. FS." She sighed. It was good they were going to meet. Now, what was she going to say to him?

Frank called in the morning to set an appointment to speak with Vanessa that afternoon. He arrived a little early and caught her finishing lunch at her desk, engrossed in the book she was reading. She jumped a little as he lightly knocked on the open door.

"I know I'm early and I can come back if you want."

"No, please come in!" Vanessa rose to greet him. "I'm glad you're here. I really shouldn't read at lunch. I'm done eating, but don't even remember what I had."

"That's a good book, then. What are you reading?"

She smiled and motioned to the cut-out figures around the room. "Well, now that I'm surrounded by these characters, I figured I should get to know them better." She held up a copy of Mary Shelley's *Frankenstein*. "I'm really enjoying it. And I was surprised that the story is much different than the old *Frankenstein* movie."

Frank reached out for the book and leafed through the pages as he spoke. "I know. In both of them, though, you've got to feel sorry for the monster. He was created, and then left to fare on his own. He looked intimidating and couldn't communicate. He's alone, trying to figure it out for himself. You can't blame him when he gets mad."

Vanessa was a little surprised by Frank's empathy with the monster. Something in his tone struck a chord with her.

"I can relate to that," she began. "It's like when I first became a manager. One day all I'm responsible for is … well, me, really. The next day, I'm supposed to be in charge. I rarely always knew how to handle things. Sometimes I wanted to stomp and growl, too. Yikes!" Then she waited.

Frank looked up at her, a frown furrowed his brow. After a moment, he spoke quietly. "I thought I was the only one who felt that way. I sure couldn't ask anyone. I figured they gave me the position cause they thought I could do it. If they found out I couldn't....."

Vanessa put her hand on his shoulder and walked with him to the chairs. He sat down with her, but his mind seemed to be elsewhere. "I remember the night after I was made manager. I was a wreck! What did I know about managing people? What had I gotten myself into? Then I thought, 'other people have done this' and calmed down. I had learned my job plus others and understand the business, so I can do this!"

"So how do you think you're doing?" Wham! She'd just put it right out there.

"Well...I thought I was really getting the hang of it. Everyone...well, almost everyone...agreed that our department had gotten off track, so I brought some structure back. People shaped up, our numbers improved and we could feel proud of our results." He shook his head, "I guess, as I look back, I came on kinda strong, but I couldn't risk looking like I didn't know what I was doing! They'd have walked all over me!"

Vanessa just nodded and Frank continued. "It was so much easier when all I had to worry about was my job. I know I overreact sometimes, but they've _got_ to do what I tell them to do! They don't know what it's like! The pressure! If we don't meet our goals, I'm responsible. If they make an error, I'm responsible. When things go wrong, I'm responsible. I have to make them respect me!"

It was clear to Vanessa now. Frank had been made a manager one day, then left on his own to be successful. He took the responsibility seriously, so he had been operating out of fear...of failure and of people judging him as he learned his way. He quickly adapted a very authoritarian style. In his eyes, the department, and therefore Scaree Costumes, was always teetering on the brink of disaster with himself as the final line of defense. Unfortunately, he had passed the fear on to the other employees. Rather than strive for success as a team, they each had begun working individually to avoid his wrath. The result was that they just quit doing much of anything. So production and motivation for improvement was down, which just raised the frustration for Frank. It was a vicious cycle!

Her reply was simple, yet powerful. "They already did."

Frank met her look, but didn't seem to understand. "They already did respect you," she continued. "They speak well of the days they worked side by side with you. When you became manager, they were glad for the renewed focus and structure."

Now he shook his head, "Not all of them."

"Of course. Change is difficult. It's important to include people in the process, keep them informed about the 'whys' of it and how they fit in. Without that, it's hard to move forward. They don't really know where they're going, so it feels more like you're pushing from behind rather than leading."

"Exactly!!" He beamed. "I never thought of it that way, but that's exactly how I feel!"

"It sounds exhausting! For everyone."

"It is! And frustrating!" Frank slouched back in the chair like he'd just finished running a race. "How can I get them behind me? Will you help me?"

Vanessa smiled. It wouldn't be all easy-going, but she had a good feeling Frank was on his way to becoming a good, maybe even great, manager.

CHAPTER 2

DRAKE ULA:

SUCKING THE LIFE OUT OF YOUR TEAM

LIGHTNING PIERCES THE DARK, gray afternoon sky. Thunder cracks like a whip, then rumbles off into the distance. Inside, the room is dim. The irregular flashes of light reveal a woman sitting motionless in a large high back chair and three ominous creatures lurking behind her. The office door opens quietly, slowly, allowing just a crack of light from the hallway at first. Then a little more. The woman tenses. The beasts are still. Seconds pass. Suddenly the room is filled with too bright, artificial light and a man's loud voice, "Aha!"

Rather than vanquish the monsters, the harsh light accentuates the demented features and menacing poses meant to instill fear. It doesn't seem to be working. The man enters the room, strolling carelessly past them without a second's hesitation.

"What are you doing?" He continues his meanderings as he speaks, "Why are you sitting in the dark?" He motions with his head towards the brutes, which his intrusion had frozen in place. "You and your friends holding a meeting?"

Disguising her annoyance with a smile, Vanessa Helsing turns her chair away from the window and faces the intruder, her colleague, Drake Ula, as he comes to rest on the corner of the imitation cherry wood desk next to her chair.

"Hello, Drake." Vanessa, known for her good nature, ignores his remarks and replies pleasantly. "I was thinking."

"Uh-oh," chuckles Drake, holding up his hands in mock surrender. "That could be dangerous!"

She notices a drain on her energy, but fights it back. "Actually, I was hoping to speak with you."

"Oh, yeah? What about?" Drake casually leafs through the mail on her desk. While he is distracted, Vanessa slowly reaches into the top drawer of her desk. Her hand finds its prize. She knows what has to be done.

Drake turns to her, and their eyes meet. His face holds the same bland combination of smug confidence, innocence and confusion she noticed the first day she had met him. Was it only a week ago?

~~~~~~~~~

Being the newcomer, Vanessa had a perfect excuse for touring the different departments. She would be "just saying hello!" Her office was near the recruiting and training departments, so she started there. As she expected, the employees were excited to talk about the Scaree Costume Company culture. Dorothy Gale, Manager of Training, was happy to show Vanessa around the classrooms. They stopped to talk in an empty hallway. "It's a unique business," she explained. "We work hard here, especially this time of year."

"*Some* people work hard here, anyway," came a disembodied voice. She looked quizzically at Dorothy who only shrugged. When Vanessa looked around to attach it to a person, the hallway was empty. Unwilling to let it go on a negative note, Vanessa countered, "I'm sure everyone here works hard." Though she waited, there was no response. Continuing the tour, Vanessa noticed that Dorothy's exuberance had diminished.

In the Accounting Department, Vanessa met Hans M. Prince. He welcomed her with a charming smile. She liked him immediately. He was new to Scaree as well, he told her, and was very happy there. "Just wait till you've been here awhile." It happened again...the voice out of nowhere. Vanessa looked around the small cubicle in a panic. The look on Hans' face reflected both boredom and annoyance. Vanessa leaned closer to him. In a whisper she asked, "Did you hear that?"

"Unfortunately," he responded with a sigh, the enthusiasm she'd just felt from him drained away. "That was Drake. He just passed by behind you."

"Who is Drake?" she asked.

"Drake Ula, Manager of Sales here at Scaree. He barges in everywhere and always has a comment...unless you actually need something from him. Then it's like you don't exist."

"He's a *Manager*?" Vanessa was incredulous. "How did that happen??" But then, she knew what she was going to hear.

"He knows the business and in many ways, he's not a bad guy. He just doesn't take his role as a leader seriously."

Vanessa changed the subject in an attempt to restore the mood that Drake's careless comment had broken. Hans spoke highly of his colleagues and their talents as well as his future at Scaree. Vanessa felt he was a very good fit for the company. She thanked Hans for his time and said her good-byes.

As Vanessa headed back towards her office, the events of the morning were running through her mind. The smell of food distracted her as she passed the cafeteria. She stopped. Whatever they were cooking smelled delicious, and she needed some time to process what she had learned so far. She decided it was time for lunch.

About half the tables were full when she entered the dining area carrying a shiny brown tray. A large ceramic bowl of soup sent up a luscious, steamy cloud. The employees had been happy to tell her that all the food was hand prepared right there in a state-of-the-art kitchen using fresh, local ingredients. Vanessa liked to eat, but didn't care much about cooking so she was looking forward to this meal as well as many others in the future.

She raised the first spoonful to her lips, but her hand froze when she heard a voice she recognized. "You should have gotten the chicken. I never eat the soup here." She raised her eyes to see a man standing over her. She didn't quite know how...or even if...she should respond. It was the owner of 'the voice'. He didn't disappear this time.

"My name is Drake. Drake Ula. Manager of Sales. Just wanted to welcome you to Scaree." His abrupt delivery didn't match the words.

"Thank you." Vanessa put down the spoon and started to introduce herself, but Drake plunged on.

"You're the new HR person. Bonita, right?"

"Vanessa." She glanced around her at the other tables. People were intently ignoring the scene playing out within a few feet of them.

"Really? I could have sworn they told me Bonita. I'll just call you Bonnie." He didn't even seem to take a breath. "I'm not sure what you do, but if you need to know anything about Sales, you can call on me or anybody on my team. They do a real good job. And if they don't, I let them know. Anyway, I'll probably see you at the weekly staff meeting this afternoon." With this parting comment he rolled his eyes, the rest of his body followed and the next thing she knew he was gone.

She looked down at her lunch and realized she didn't feel very hungry now. She felt tired.

She finished about half of her soup before she pulled herself from the plastic seat in the cafeteria and headed towards the comfort of her office. She was intercepted by Cindy Rella, the receptionist. "Hello, Ms. Helsing. The weekly staff meeting is in Conference Room Boo. It starts in 15 minutes. I know everyone wants to meet you."

Vanessa let out a resigned sigh, then caught herself. That wasn't like her!! She hoped Cindy hadn't noticed! "Thank you, Cindy. I'm looking forward to meeting them as well." As she made her way to the conference room, she gave herself an internal shaking and a stern talking-to. She was a professional. She knew how important it was to be a positive role model. Her mentor had always reminded her. 'When you accept a leadership role, you need to be aware and demonstrate leadership behaviors.' She'd slipped on her first day, but she was back on her game now!

Only a few people sat scattered around the large table when she got there. Vanessa greeted each of them and introduced herself. They began talking quietly among themselves. When Drake came in, he took a seat next to Vanessa. He did not speak. His Blackberry made an immediate entrance, however. Self-importantly, Drake immersed himself in the intensely intriguing messages he found there, to the exclusion of all other sensory stimulus. The seats in the room filled up yet his focus never wavered except to make a "tsk" of dismay or sigh impatiently. Mrs. Scaree and the CEO Freddie Katz entered the room. "Thank you for coming today," began Mr. Katz. "Before we talk Scaree business, I'd like to introduce Vanessa Helsing. Vanessa comes to us with an impressive combination of expertise and experience. Her specialty is Employee Relations. We all know we have a great team here. I am confident that under Vanessa's guidance, it will grow and thrive. Welcome, Vanessa." Even though she felt uncomfortable in the small spotlight, Vanessa appreciated the kind words. She saw smiles around the table and there was brief applause. Except for Drake, who was checking his Blackberry. It shouldn't have bothered her, but it took a little of her pride in the moment.

Mr. Katz continued, "Will each of you introduce yourself, please?" Vanessa could not help but notice Drake exaggeratedly look at his watch. His behavior continued throughout the meeting.

~~~~~~~~

At the end of the day, Vanessa liked to sit quietly and review her day. This one had given her lots to think about. She had met many of her new co-workers and had the opportunity to see the owner and CEO interact with the management members. Her initial impression was quite positive...except for Drake Ula. Just the thought of him made her tired.

Over the next few days, Vanessa made it a point to visit all the different departments at Scaree Costume Company. On Thursday, she was talking with a member of the sales team in his office when Drake entered and began speaking, all in one motion. "I just got your vacation request, Jack. This isn't a good time." Jack looked embarrassed and surprised. Vanessa stood to leave, "I'll come back later, Jack. I appreciate your time." Drake hadn't even notice her there. He frowned a little as he took in the scene. He obviously decided not to comment on her presence, only making a dismissive motion for her to sit down, "This will only take a minute. So, I'll reschedule that vacation time for ...I don't know... I'll get back to you."

Jack must have been momentarily stunned. Drake had turned to leave when he spoke up. "But I submitted that request a month ago so I can be there when Jill's mother leaves. You approved it. Remember? We just had a baby!"

Drake rolled his eyes. "Remember? I let them have a baby party for you, didn't I? Even though it's weird to have a baby party for a man." Drake held up his arms in surrender. "But, if you insist, take the time! Don't worry about the burden on everyone while you're enjoying your vacation." His parting words were, "Keep your phone on!"

Vanessa felt dazed. She'd just witnessed a hit and run! "Is he always like that?"

"You mean abrupt, condescending and detached? Only on his good days." Jack tried to laugh it off, but Vanessa wanted to know. "Have you tried talking to him?"

"I've tried. It doesn't do any good to say anything to him. He's got lots of ways of saying 'who cares what you think?' Things like 'I'm just being real with you.', 'You need to learn to take criticism'. And my favorite, 'It is what it is.'" Jack made a face like he'd just tasted something bad. "Usually he's doing something else while you're talking anyway. Why bother?" His shoulders shrugged, then slumped. The body language of resignation.

"Anyway, we still get the work done and he thinks he's 'motivating' us. He's right, too. He's motivated lots of us to not want to work!" His eyes opened wide as he realized his slip. "Oops, I shouldn't have told you that."

"Don't worry," she calmed, "Frankly, I don't blame you." Then she smiled, "Oops, I shouldn't have said that." She was glad to see a spark of humor back in Jack's eyes.

~~~~~~~~

The next day she made a point to return to the Sales Department. She wanted to learn more about Drake Ula. Vanessa had witnessed the signs of apathy throughout all departments, but here it seemed the most intense and pervasive. Here was the source, she thought. Drake's office door was open, but he was nowhere to be seen. She asked a woman who was working in the area where she might find him. She shrugged as she replied in a dead-serious tone, "Do something wrong. He'll find *you* in a hurry."

Vanessa returned to Drake's empty office. There were plaques and photos on the walls. She moved closer to read them. "Number 1 Sales Team", "Performance Champions – Scaree Sales Team", Scaree Softball Team - Sales. All were team awards or pictures except for the last one. They say a picture is worth 1,000 words. Well, this one was speaking loud and clear to Vanessa. It was a picture of Drake at the Annual Scaree Costume Ball. Posing for the camera, he made a very convincing Dracula.

"That's it," she said aloud. She thought of the people she had met this week. She remembered Dorothy, Hans, Jack and others. She had witnessed enthusiasm, pride and motivation drained from them. There was her own exhaustion and lapse of professionalism. "He's an Office Vampire!" Her mind pictured him moving freely among the offices and cubicles, his words and behaviors sucking the life out of the unwary employees. They didn't stand a chance. "I've got to stop him!"

A plan began to form in her mind. Vanessa glanced at her watch. There was plenty of time. She found pen and paper quickly on Drake's neat desk, scribbled a few words and left the note on his chair. It didn't take long for her to gather what she needed, then she settled into her office to wait.

~~~~~~~~~

Vanessa was confident he would not knock, so she sat ready. She hadn't had to wait long.

Now, close enough to smell garlic from today's spaghetti lunch on his breath, Vanessa looks into his eyes and prepares to confront Drake Ula. Keeping her composure, she stands. At the same time, she slowly lifts her hand from the desk drawer. The time is now… but she remains determined to be professional.

"Drake, this is difficult for me to say, and I'm sure it will be difficult for you to hear. I want to talk to you because I want you to be successful." Drake begins to look suspicious. "You have a great talent for sales at Scaree Costumes. You can be proud that you have moved up through the company into management. I want to help you build your skills to help you be a more successful leader for the people on your team."

"Good luck improving perfection," Drake quips dryly. That's it! No more kid gloves! Vanessa makes her move.

She thrusts her arm towards Drake, holding a small mirror in her hand like a shield. She wants to reveal him. Unsure of the response she expects, she braces herself. He doesn't cry out or shrink back in fear. True to Drake form, he is oblivious. He calmly reaches out, takes the mirror from her outstretched hand and proceeds to examine himself. "Oh, thanks. Do I have something in my teeth?" Vanessa sighs in exasperation. She snatches the mirror back and tosses it aside.

"I was going to use it as a metaphor...that as managers we must be willing to look at ourselves and our behaviors...but never mind, now..." Drake's blank look told her she was going to have to be brutal. "Drake, in just one week, you have alternately ignored me and invaded my personal space. I have stood by as you made demeaning, sarcastic comments, taken credit for the work of others, interrupted conversations and subtly disrupted meetings. And you still don't get my name right! These behaviors communicate disrespect, which in turn, alienates and demotivates people. Then it spreads. It's toxic to a company."

"Toxic?? I think you're overreacting, Vanessa," oozes Drake, emphasizing her name as he reads it from a piece of her mail before tossing it back on her desk. "Everyone knows I don't mean anything by it. Loosen up! So, I don't coddle people. They get motivated every two weeks, right?"

"It happens gradually," she continues, undaunted, as if he hasn't spoken. "Every negative comment or behavior drains away a little bit of enthusiasm and trust, the foundations of productivity.

"Grown ups know what they need to do. If they mess up, I tell 'em. I get the job done," he replies smugly. "The proof is in the facts and numbers."

"What if I could show you some facts and numbers that show you how to get it done more effectively?" Vanessa knew she was on the right track. She had seen the plaque in his office for President's Club Award for top sales. "You were awarded for top sales growth for the past 5 years?" He nods cautiously.

Vanessa moves to her bookcase and retrieves several books she had staged there. None of them are large, but obviously well read, adorned with colorful bookmarks. Prepared, she opens the first one and points to a highlighted paragraph. "Here's one from Zig Ziglar. Hard facts that show that communication, respect and trust are the foundations of a successful employee/manager work environment *and* it impacts sales, every time. It comes from positive reinforcement, knowing your employees, personal interactions and regular feedback. The most effective behavior to get the best results." She studies his face for a response, but still isn't sure. With a sigh, she closes the book and holds it out to Drake. "Take it. Read it. You'll see."

Drake reluctantly reaches out and takes the book. At first she thought it would be a brief glance, but to her surprise he settles himself into the chair and proceeds to immerse himself in the text. A little bewildered, Vanessa moves back to her desk and begins working. The quiet is broken by an occasional sound from Drake...."huh", "OK", "hmmm". It is almost five o'clock when he closes the cover. He thoughtfully peruses the other books she had produced. After a few moments, he spoke. It hardly sounded like Drake. "I haven't been doing any of the things that really *work* to motivate people. I never asked to be a manager, but I didn't try to learn how to be a good one either. I just imitated managers I'd had or known over the years. Some of them I couldn't stand, either!"

The sun was going down, but Vanessa wasn't afraid to stand beside Drake. The vampire was gone, at least for now. "You can be a great manager...if you want to be. It will take some time and effort, but I have confidence in you." Drake looked hopeful for a moment, then almost afraid. In a hushed tone, he said, "There are others, you know." He motioned with his eyes, "Out there."

Vanessa knew what he meant. Her thoughts flew over the maze of cubicles, workspaces and offices outside her office door. In her mind, she saw the people who actually were the Scaree Costume Company. The great people she had met and the many she had yet to know. It wouldn't take long for her to find out that he was right.

CHAPTER 3

IAN VEESABLE:

YOU CAN BE TOO HANDS OFF

Locked again! Margie Franklin shakes the door handle in frustration. This is the third time this week that she has come to get something from the supply room and found it locked. The fact that it is actually *supposed* to be kept locked at all times does nothing to mitigate her annoyance. She's the only person with a key...isn't she?

Hans M. Prince is met by the rich smell of freshly brewed coffee when he enters the breakroom. Until recently, it had seemed that he alone was capable of creating the coveted liquid. Surprisingly, no one has taken credit for being the Mystery Brewer, nor has he seen anyone. Hans pours himself a large, steamy cup, appreciatively sniffing the scent. Just before taking the first sip, he raises the cup in a salute, "Thank you, whoever you are!"

All around the Scaree Costume Company, employees have been noticing small, unexplained occurrences. Letters and packages which often sit idly in the "Outgoing Mail" for days are now mysteriously transported to the mailroom. Needed supplies appear in the copy room and restrooms. Reports are filed. At first, people were just happy that things were getting done. Soon, delight gave way to curiosity which is now uneasiness. Who could be doing these things and why??

Vanessa Helsing first became aware of the phenomena by accident. She overheard Cindy Rella, the Receptionist, and another employee animatedly discussing what they called the Scaree Ghost. (Vanessa was not averse to eavesdropping on public conversations, this one being held in the main lobby of Scaree.) It seems that upon arriving at her desk this morning, Cindy discovered a new call log process on her desk.

"It's a good process," Cindy conceded, "It's like the one you got last week. Where are they coming from? This is getting creepy."

Vanessa could not see them and did not recognize the man's voice that answered, "I'm sure there is a reasonable explanation, but it would be ok with me if a ghost did *my* month-end report."

They laughed, but Vanessa caught a note of apprehension in Cindy's voice. She stepped out to speak with them, but Cindy was on the phone. She just caught sight of a man's coat as he disappeared into Conference Room Boo. She decided to investigate this herself.

Vanessa was the Sr. Manager of Human Resources at Scaree Costume Company, and as such, had a responsibility to the employees to maintain a safe, productive, successful work environment. That was one of the reasons it was important for her to keep her ears open. She learned a lot that way. That was how she came to be in the Accounting Department this morning. Vanessa had determined that the majority of Scaree Ghost stories originated here. This had raised her level of concern, as the Accounting Department was the last place people wanted to hear about mysterious appearances or disappearances! She was meeting Hans Prince, one of the newer accountants. They had become acquainted her first week at Scaree during another investigation. She hoped he would be talkative.

They met in the break room near his cubicle, enjoying a cup of coffee as they talked. "Yup," he said as he tipped his cup to take a noisy drink. Hans was a slurper. "This was one of the first things I noticed. A ghost that makes darn good coffee first thing in the morning. I even tried coming in early, just to see if I could catch a glimpse, but …nothing."

Vanessa looked at him over the rim of her cup as she took her first sip. It *was* good. "You don't really think it's a ghost, do you?"

"I'd relish the irony," he said with a half smile. "A haunted costume manufacturer. Anyway, you already vanquished a vampire here."

That set her thinking, "And there was never a *real* vampire. Sooo, maybe I need to take a new perspective. No one admits to doing anything, right? Perhaps it's someone we don't know."

"A stranger breaks in to Scaree to make coffee, mail packages and generally make sure that tasks get done?" Hans grinned at the thought, "Kind of 'reverse vandalism', eh? Interesting idea."

"Not a stranger, just not someone we know. I'll have to think about it." Vanessa washed her cup as Hans poured himself another.

As she was leaving, he implored, "Please don't scare him…or her away." Laughing, she opened the door and stepped into the hallway where she crashed head-on into a man. She had barely had time to see him walking quickly towards her, head down, eyes on the floor. Vanessa hadn't had time to react and he hadn't slowed down. They were both temporarily stunned. The man spoke first, "I'm terribly sorry. I hope you're not hurt."

Vanessa patted herself as if checking for injuries, then realized she no longer had the empty cup in her hand. Looking down, she saw it on the floor in three pieces. "I think it's totaled," she said, mock seriously.

He picked up the broken cup, "I sure hope I have my insurance card. Should we call the police?"

"Please don't. I pulled out in front of you."

"I may have been speeding." They both laughed.

She held out her hand, "Vanessa Helsing"

"My apologies, again, Ms. Helsing. I'm Ian...Ian Veesable, and I am also running late for an appointment. Maybe we'll run into each other again sometime." Just as he turned to go, the door to the breakroom opened. She just missed bumping into Hans.

"This is a dangerous intersection," she quipped. Hans looked confused. "What does Ian do here in Accounting?" She nodded down the hall behind Hans where she could still see Ian.

Hans turned to look, but Ian had just turned the corner. "Who is Ian? I don't see anyone. There's no Ian in our department. We didn't even rank a manager until about a month ago. Nobody has ever talked to us about it and we haven't met him. The word is that he's 'getting acclimated.'" He shook his head. "I don't know what that means, but hope he shows up soon."

"Is there a problem? Why do you want him here soon?"

Hans looked as if he regretted his words. "Nothing, really," he began. "It's just...well, without one leader, people start kind of doing whatever they want. It makes it harder to work together. For example, we have four supervisors. They have different personalities and priorities, so what one sup says is important today, the sup working tomorrow may say, 'Why are you doing that? Do this.'" Hans shrugged his shoulders. "I'm not sure if that makes any sense to you, but it's confusing and unproductive."

Vanessa knew exactly what he was talking about and told him so. "I understand perfectly. It happens even when people have the best of intentions. You're right that any team is more effective with a leader." They said their goodbyes and turned in opposite directions.

Vanessa began walking again, only to stop a short way down the hallway. She stood in front of a closed door. The sign next to it said, Department Manager. As Hans had said, the Accounting Department had been without a manager for some time, but they had recently hired a very qualified person. The department ran well because Scaree had capable people like Hans, but every team is enhanced with a good leader. Vanessa made a mental note to come back later.

As Sr. Manager of HR, one would think that she knew every person at Scaree. In fact, Vanessa herself had only been at the company about two months and was still learning all the job titles and positions there. Manufacturing, selling and distributing quality costumes was actually a complex business, and Scaree Costume Company was one of the largest and oldest.

Nevertheless, Vanessa felt badly that she had not met the new Manager of Accounting. She looked in the company directory for a name, but the space was still blank. She decided to stop by tomorrow morning to say hello.

As she was leaving for the evening, Vanessa rode the elevator with Drake Ula. She and Drake had gone from being adversaries, in a way, to allies. After a draining intervention (pun intended), Drake had changed his management style. He was now instrumental in developing the company's new rewards and recognition program.

They spoke of the newest recognition initiative that was to be rolled out to all the managers this week. "There will be a few tough sells," he sighed. "Mainly because of me. You know how oblivious I had become."

"But you were willing to change, and I'm sure you will be able to convince veterans and new managers as well." That prompted her to ask, "By the way, who is the new Manager of Accounting?"

Scratching his chin, Drake thought for a moment, then shook his head. "He's been on management conference calls, but not at meetings. He's got some good ideas for the department," said Drake. "Now that you mention it, I've gotten emails from him. He doesn't have voicemail." He looked at Vanessa with curiosity. "What's up?"

The elevator doors opened. Vanessa replied honestly as they exited, "I'm not sure anything is up."

"If there is anything I can help you with, just let me know. I owe you, y'know. Your advice has made my life much easier."

"I'm glad to hear that, Drake," she smiled, "but you don't owe me. You've done it yourself." She waved over her shoulder as they parted ways on the sidewalk outside the building.

~~~~~~~~~~

The aroma of the brewing coffee was the first thing Vanessa noticed when she arrived in Accounting early the next morning, but the breakroom was empty. She looked down the hallway. The manager's office door was open. She stopped to knock on the doorframe, but that room, too, was empty. Well, he must be close.

She was debating going back to her office when the employees began arriving. Then she saw Ian. He had displayed kindness and a sense of humor when she'd met him yesterday so she was surprised to see him pass the other employees without speaking. She was even more surprised when he entered the manager's office and closed the door.

Vanessa approached the office. The closed door did not welcome visitors and the solid deep brown of the imitation mahogany door screamed, Keep Out!

Undeterred, she raised her hand and knocked. There was no response. She had just seen him go in there! She knocked again, waited just a moment, then turned knob and entered. The office was dim, but Vanessa clearly saw Ian's face. He looked terrified!

"Hello, Ian." She closed the door behind her and walked closer. Now he just looked guilty. Her voice revealed curiosity, not accusation. "Why are you in here and why didn't you answer when I knocked?" At the same moment, she noticed the photo on the credenza behind him. It showed Ian with a lovely woman and two small children. Suddenly, it all made sense.

"Ian, *you're* the new Manager of Accounting!" He just nodded. "Oh, Ian, you're not the Scaree Ghost, you're the Invisible Man! You have been here for over a month and your own team doesn't know who you are! Tell me what is going on!!"

He slumped back in his chair as he spoke. "The people in this department know their jobs and do them well. I figure that I should just stay out of their way and let them do it. I'm a 'hands-off manager'. They should have the freedom to do their job without me looking over their shoulder."

Ian was utterly sincere, "I don't mind that people don't know who I am. I don't need any credit for what I do."

Vanessa's irritation with Ian drained out of her. "Ian, people *want* to connect with their leader and each other.

It makes them feel part of the whole. What you see as a 'hands-off' management style is usually interpreted by the employees as 'you don't care'."

"But I do care!" Ian sat up straight. "I have been exploring new processes and technology that are more effective and make their jobs easier as well as regular training to keep them up to date. I have reviewed files and completed all the required paperwork should we be audited. We have some work to do, but the whole team has done a wonderful job of maintaining the integrity of the department and the company in the absence of a manager. They really don't need me."

Vanessa moved around the desk to stand next to Ian. "What they need from you is exactly what you just told me. They need you to be an advocate for them, to guide them to grow in their jobs and help them direct and focus their energies. And they need you to recognize their hard work, reward the results and encourage their efforts. To do all that, you need to *talk to them!* I know you can do it, because you did it with me yesterday. In just a few moments, I saw your calm sense of humor, good manners and resolve to keep your commitments. Thinking back, in that brief time, I decided I liked and respected you. See how easy it could be?"

Rather than looking pleased at the encouragement, Ian looked even more despairing, "I've really messed up! How will I be able to face these people now? They think I've been avoiding them...that I don't respect *them.*" He leaned on the desk and held his head in his hands. "I thought I was doing the right thing. This is a nightmare! I wish I *was* invisible!"

Vanessa was undaunted. Now that she understood, she was confident that Ian could be a great manager. "It's not as bad as that," she soothed. "You can begin right now." She walked to the door and opened it wide. "This is the beginning of your 'open door policy'," she said smiling. Ian looked at her skeptically. "Now let's go out and walk around a little. Did you know that Hans is thrilled that someone else is willing to make coffee? It's a gesture that means a lot to him. Just think, when he finds out it's you... ."

"But won't they think it's weird...that I just show up?"

"You might start with something like, 'Hello, I'm Ian. I'm sorry it's taken me awhile to meet you. Tell me about yourself.' When they find you are sincerely interested in them and ready to move forward, I'm sure they'll be right there with you."

Ian's demeanor had changed. "You're right. I want to work *with* these people. I admire them and really *do* want to get to know them. I know we can build an even more successful team. Suddenly it doesn't seem so complicated!"

He stood up and walked towards Vanessa where she stood by the door. "I think I'll see if Hans can spare a few minutes to have a cup of coffee with me." He hesitated. "Are you free to coach...I mean...join me?"

Then he laughed. "That really *was* transparent. What I meant to say is, 'will you come along and help me get started?'"

Vanessa knew Ian would be fine on his own. "Sure. It sounds like fun."

He faced her. As if he had read her thoughts, "Thanks, Vanessa. You're right, y'know. I could do this alone, but I appreciate having your support."

He started to close the door behind them, then stopped. Looking pleased with himself, he pushed it open all the way.

CHAPTER 4

HEIDI JECKLE:

WORKING ON THE RIGHT FORMULA

Brenda's heart was pounding as she dialed the phone. She knew there were only a few moments to make the call without anyone knowing. Hands trembling, she misdialed twice before it went through. One ring. Two. 'Please be at your desk', she thought. Three rings. Brenda looked nervously over her shoulder. Four rings. "Hello. You have reached Vanessa Helsing, Sr. Manager of Human Resources." Damn voicemail! What should she do? Her mind raced, then she decided. At the tone she quickly left her name and number and hung up. Leaning against the desk, Brenda felt like she'd just run a race. Shaking her head, she gave herself a firm talking-to. "For crying out loud, Brenda, you're not doing anything wrong. Why are you acting so guilty?"

"Brenda. Are you all right?" Instinct kicked in and she went rigid at the sound of the voice behind her. Then, identifying the gentle tone, she relaxed and turned to face Heidi. "Oh, my goodness, Brenda!" The look communicated genuine concern. "You don't look well."

Brenda knew it was a brief reprieve, but was glad for it. "I ate something spicy for lunch. I'll be fine." She quickly excused herself past a bewildered Heidi, patting authentic perspiration from her brow. Hopefully Vanessa would call her back soon. It could just have easily been Dr. Jeckle.

• • •

Vanessa Helsing enjoyed her job. Interesting people and projects. This morning, for instance, she survived an attack by a werewolf.

She had been sitting idly in a meeting, half listening to a report on sales and advertising when the beast physically exploded into the room. Her seat, carefully selected for its proximity to the door, now made her the closest target. Her first thought was, "It's not real. It's not real." Vanessa repeated the mantra in her mind as the man-sized animal moved closer.

Contradicting her thoughts, her senses absorbed the unintelligible growling and mewling, the tangled fur and sour smell. "It's not real," she affirmed in a whisper this time. His sunken, bloodshot eyes locked with hers. Others in the room sat wide-eyed and still as the monster's heavy steps moved him closer and closer to where Vanessa sat paralyzed in her chair. Suddenly, as if hearing a sound, the werewolf stopped, then quickly bounded from the room without a backward glance at his potential victim.

Vanessa realized she'd been holding her breath. She closed her eyes and exhaled.

Spontaneous applause and relieved laughter spread through the crowd. "Just another day at work," someone behind her quipped. Looking around the room, Vanessa could tell that several others had been startled as well.

Shaking her head with a relieved smile, she said, 'I have to admit, I'm still getting used to these Product Research & Development meetings!" There is more laughter along with nods of agreement.

A woman wearing a white lab jacket replaced the previous speaker at the front of the room with a friendly handshake, then addressed the room with a smile. "Thank you all for that valuable...feedback!" There was some appreciative laughter, then a brief wave of her arm, summoned the werewolf back into the room and to her side. Another wave sent the beast loping around the room, subdued, but in character, sniffing sleeves and peering intently into faces. "As most of you know, my name is Dr. Heidi Jeckle. I'm the leader of the Research and Development Department here at Scaree Costume Company. I am very pleased with your initial response to the enhanced Werewolf costume that will be featured in an upcoming television series."

Dr. Heidi Jeckle continued her presentation, the picture of professionalism and composure.

After the meeting, Vanessa returned to her office and retrieved the voice message from Brenda. It was odd, to be sure. In it, Brenda was whispering and out of breath which created an air of desperation in the simple request, "Please, call me." Vanessa remembered Brenda Beakers well. They had met at one of the new product meetings, similar to the one today. Brenda worked in the Research and Development Department and hadn't seemed like someone who would overreact. With that thought in mind, Vanessa continued to review the messages.

As the next one began, she immediately recognized the voice. "Hello, Vanessa. This is Heidi. Heidi Jeckle. I hope you enjoyed the meeting today. Seeing you gave me an idea that I'd like to bounce off you. Would you please give me a call when you get a moment? I look forward to talking with you." Darn, she didn't leave her extension.

Vanessa turned on her computer to access the corporate phone directory.

Of course, new emails popped up. She couldn't resist looking. Though there were several, she noticed that the last four were from Heidi Jeckle... sent within 5 minutes of each other. She opened the last one and was startled by the large red font. "Don't you respond to your email??? I said I need to talk to you ASAP!!"

Yikes! The phone message hadn't sounded urgent at all.

Vanessa opened the other emails from Heidi. They had escalated in tone from friendly request to heated demand. Interestingly, her signature had also changed. The first one was signed, Heidi. The next was Heidi Jeckle, then Dr. Jeckle, culminating with no signature at all on the last. What had she missed? It had only been about 20 minutes since the end of that meeting!

She was definitely intrigued. First Brenda, then Heidi. Both in Research and Development. Vanessa decided she'd better call Heidi first. Dialing the number she'd found in the directory, Vanessa realized she was bracing herself. She was already anticipating the tone of the conversation based on the last email. There was a ray of hope when she thought the call was going to roll over to voicemail, but just then a bright voice came on the line. "Hello, Heidi Jeckle."

"Hello, Dr. Jeckle. This is Vanessa Helsing returning your call."

"Vanessa! You sound so stressed!" The surprised tone caught Vanessa off guard. "I hope the werewolf didn't upset you too much!"

"Noooo," she replied cautiously.

Heidi sounded excited. "Didn't he look great though? Brenda has done a fabulous job on the new fur. It makes all the difference. Now, what can I do for you?"

Vanessa frowned. "I'm returning your call."

"Oh, that's right…silly me! Thank you so much. I know you're busy, but I'd like to ask you to participate in a teambuilding session I'm having tomorrow with my department. I've been here about six months." Heidi spoke more quietly now. "To be honest, we started off well, but lately, productivity has been steadily declining. People seem to have lost enthusiasm and motivation. I hope this will help."

A team builder in Research & Development with a leader who sounded angry one minute and effusive the next. Her mind's response was "This, I've gotta see!"

Fortunately, her lips were more tactful. "Thank you, Heidi. Of course I'll be there."

After getting the details from Heidi on tomorrow's activities, Vanessa disconnected the line and immediately dialed the number Brenda left in her message.

Brenda answered the phone on the second ring, sounding quite professional and calm, much unlike the phone message. The phone system automatically identified callers, so Brenda spoke without prelude, "Thank you for calling me back, Vanessa. I don't know if you remember me…"

"I do, Brenda," Vanessa assured her, "your special project is to improve the synthetic fur. The presentation was very interesting and I saw the result today at the meeting. Everyone was quite impressed with your results."

Vanessa felt Brenda blush through the phone line. "Yeah, well, our werewolf will last 50 years if you take care of it"

"That's great...but I'll bet that's not why you called me." Vanessa projected a reassuring tone and smile in her voice. "What can I do for you?'

"I'm sorry I sounded so frantic in my message," she began. "I'd just come from a meeting, and I felt like I was going crazy! I'm better now."

"Are you sure? Would you like me to come to your office so we can talk?"

"NO!" It was a quick and emphatic reply. "I mean, no, thank you. Vanessa, I feel silly, but it's been happening more and more often."

"What has?"

"It's hard to explain, really," Brenda began slowly. "Well, take today for instance. I had finished the fur part of the project so Heidi....Dr. Jeckle, told me to be prepared to present at today's team meeting on the application to wigs. She said it was a priority, and I would be the featured presenter."

Brenda paused. "That sounds great," Vanessa offered in support.

"Yeah." Brenda's tone was sarcastic. "Until I got there. When Heidi came in and saw me setting up, she went ballistic. We call it 'going Dr. Jeckle' 'cause when she goes off it's not at all like the person who first took over the department, Heidi. We all liked working with Heidi. Anyway, in front of everyone, she scolded me for not keeping up to date. She said that a memo had gone out designating that more realistic wounds were the new priority. I felt about 2 inches tall."

Vanessa cringed in sympathy.

"I couldn't believe I'd missed the communication!! After slinking back to my office, I read the memo. It had come out about 1 hour prior to the meeting, while I was busy preparing."

Before Vanessa could respond, Brenda continued. "And I'm not the only one. We all understand being flexible, but there are times when we are sitting in a meeting that was called to discuss one thing, and the entire meeting focuses on a totally different topic! Priorities shift overnight. She asks for detailed outlines of what we're working on, then still asks us, as if she doesn't read what we send her." Brenda was on a roll now. "Oh! All items submitted for publication require her approval, but she must be continually prodded to respond. Then when she finally does give the ok, we barely make the deadline. Then we're needled for waiting until the last minute! It makes a person feel insane!!"

Vanessa could only imagine Brenda's frustration. Her sigh must have carried through the line for Brenda sighed herself and said, "I'm sorry I called you. I know there's probably nothing you can do. Maybe it's just me."

"I'm glad you shared this with me, Brenda," Vanessa began. "Have you talked to Heidi about your feelings?"

"I would be OK with talking to Heidi. I like her, you see. I don't want to cause her trouble. None of us do, but Dr. Jeckle seems to be in the office more often than Heidi these days."

Brenda's voice sounded as tired as Vanessa suddenly felt. It took all her energy to sound enthusiastic as she talked about participating in the team event the next day, but it was worth it to hear the light in Brenda's voice. "Thank you, Vanessa. I'm confident that you'll know how to handle this."

Vanessa hung up the phone, wondering what she was getting in to. She would find out soon enough.

Vanessa arrived at the R & D Department promptly at 8 AM. Heidi had stressed the time, so Vanessa was surprised when she was not there yet. Brenda was there as were her colleagues. None of them seemed surprised to be there without the person who had called the meeting.

Vanessa took the opportunity to meet and talk with members of Heidi's team. Without probing, she learned that the others waiting there for Heidi felt much as Brenda did, sharing similar anecdotes. Actually, Brenda was the most optimistic! There was an aura of tension. Vanessa recognized that they were appraising the situation, waiting for Heidi to set the initial tone.

It was an almost giddy Heidi who came panting through the doorway, laughing and apologizing. She held two bags of warm donuts over her head, declaring them as a peace offering. She surprised Vanessa by opening the bags and offering donuts to each person in turn along with a personal greeting.

When she came to Vanessa, Heidi spoke quietly. "Thank you for coming today. I hope this will help us. But if you see something, don't hesitate to tell me about it. I mean that." Vanessa recognized the sincerity in Heidi's face as she hoped for a magic solution to her team's deteriorating performance. Vanessa gave her a smile of encouragement and as a gesture of support, selected a chocolate glazed donut from the bag.

Hopefully, Vanessa joined Heidi, Brenda and the others as the facilitator kicked off the teambuilding session. Then she watched as they tirelessly tried to meet Heidi's expectations. She could see why Brenda had questioned her sanity. Heidi encouraged them to be creative, work as a team and have fun as they tackled the challenges, then began to criticize, micromanage and even pull rank. In one exercise after another, Vanessa felt helpless as Dr. Jeckle continually threw up roadblocks until the team's motivation was obliterated. They asked her suggestion and went with it. When it was successful, Heidi rejoiced and called it a team effort as the others silently looked on. Soon no one wanted to even express an opinion. Oblivious to her contribution to their reticence, Heidi chided them for being indecisive. The facilitator's subtle feedback fell on deaf ears. And on it went.

By the end of the day, Heidi's goal of a united, excited team was probably even farther away. During the subdued "awards ceremony", the enthusiasm seemed forced and artificial. The highlight appeared when the facilitator declared the day complete. Vanessa sighed as she watched him pack his few remaining props and head for the door without talking with Heidi.

"Well?" Heidi's voice interrupted her thoughts. "See what I mean? They don't respect me! I don't know what else to do with them! Every day I go home exhausted. I never expected managing to be so tiring."

In her mind, Vanessa shook her head in despair. She wasn't surprised, but she was also at a loss on how to proceed. Even being on the edge of Heidi's management style flip-flops all day had given her a dull headache. Just as that thought went through her mind, Vanessa had a moment of inspiration.

"Being a new manager can be frustrating," she began cautiously.

"I've been Acting Manager of R & D for a year," replied Heidi. "That's not new. I thought I'd have my style figured out by now."

There was an interesting insight. "Style?"

"Well, I've had to figure this out on my own, y'know. One day I'm Heidi, New Products Researcher with some career aspirations, and the next thing I know I'm the manager of the department…acting manager, to be exact. I replaced Dr. Morgan. He was kind of a jerk, but brilliant."

"You must have demonstrated that you could handle the position or you wouldn't have been promoted."

"That's what Dr. Morgan said. He's also the one who taught me how to be The Manager. Capital T. Capital M. Sometimes I forget and am Heidi. Then I remember that I have to be The Manager. I have to get tough, make decisions that make the company successful. That's my job."

Vanessa thought she had gotten to the root of it all. "So when you think about it, you act the way you think a manager should act. It's like being cast in the role of 'Manager' with an incomplete script and no director."

Heidi had been getting a drink from the cooler. She stopped, paused for a second, then turned to Vanessa. She looked surprised. "That's it! That's why this is so draining! I'm not being myself and leading my team, I'm using someone else's definition and managing them."

Vanessa sat quietly as Heidi spoke her thoughts aloud, almost as if she were telling a story. Heidi was holding herself spellbound!

"I know they are capable and dependable, so I leave them to do their work. Then, as I sit in my office or in a meeting, I feel the 'Manager' taking over. The manager needs to be in charge, know what they are doing or criticize their work... to motivate them to work harder." This statement was followed by a small snort of sarcasm.

"Oh my gosh...I'm literally an Acting Manager!" As powerful as an incantation, those words seemed to break the spell. Heidi clapped her hands. "What a relief!"

Then she stopped, wide-eyed. "They must think I'm crazy! They're great people and I've made them miserable! How can I fix this?"

Vanessa smiled. "I think you know the answer to that, too, Heidi."

She was right. "I can hardly wait 'til tomorrow to talk to the team. I get it! Managing people doesn't have to be so difficult! I'm going to be the person who was promoted to manager! Me, not some dark side of me, just me!" She hugged Vanessa. "You're a genius, Vanessa, thank you!"

Vanessa smiled. Heidi practically danced out of the large conference room. "A genius" when in reality, she had hardly spoken a word. As usual, Heidi had the insight to resolve her own issues when she took another perspective. Vanessa would help as well. Just in case The Manager popped up again.

Are you a Monst-ager? To make this determination, let's look at a correlation for motivation and awareness.

– Motivation +	
Quadrant 1 - High Awareness, Low Motivation	Quadrant 2 – High Awareness, High Motivation
Quadrant 3 – Low Awareness, Low Motivation	Quadrant 4 – Low Awareness, High Motivation

Quadrant 1. From an employee standpoint, the worst managers will fall here. Unfortunately, poor management behaviors such as intimidation and fear can actually generate desired results....temporarily. These managers are highly aware of their behaviors and the impact they have on their team, but are unmotivated to make any changes. These managers are so scary, they can give you bad dreams.

Quadrant 2. The best managers are in this quadrant. They are invested in the team and themselves. These managers strive to be aware and continually improving their own skills in working with their team to get continually improving results. Not scary at all.

Quadrants 3 and 4 are where you'll find Monst-agers.

Quadrant 3. These managers usually have good technical skills which are the foundation of their promotion. They do not view themselves as team leaders, so are not motivated to develop managerial skills. They may tend to forget about the team and continue to primarily focus on the job.

Quadrant 4. They want to be good to great managers. Though they may study management techniques, they lack basic awareness of their own behaviors and/or the impact. Without this discernment, these managers tend to fall back on behaviors they have seen or experienced through other managers (good or bad) to define management behaviors.

Frank Stein: Basic Scare Tactics

Monstrous Beliefs

- If I don't yell at them, they won't take me seriously.
- Fear equals respect.
- Consequences are important. If something goes wrong, someone must be held responsible.

Employee Perceptions

If I try something new or think for myself, I'll get in 'trouble'.

I can't please this person.

He/she wouldn't act that way if they respected me.

Do they know how ridiculous they seem when they yell and act out?

Vanessa's Tips

Focus on solutions, not blame or punishment. A calm and composed approach to solving problems communicates a leader's confidence in his/her ability – and the team's ability – to find a solution.

Accountability vs. Blame – one is focused on the outcome, the other on the people involved. Blame does nothing to find a resolution.

Losing one's temper and/or composure with employees or customers is unprofessional and unacceptable.

DRAKE ULA:
SUCKING THE LIFE OUT OF YOUR TEAM

"VAMPIRE" MANAGER BELIEFS

- If I'm nice to my team members, they will take advantage of me.
- Positive recognition or rewards are a bribe. Pay is incentive enough for performance.
- Negative recognition works – people can be shamed into performance.
- Fun in the workplace is an unnecessary distraction. If people are laughing, they must not be working.
- Talking about topics unrelated to work is a waste of time. Work is primary obligation of employees (no room for outside life at work).
- It's important to place blame when things go wrong.

DRAINING STATEMENTS

"I don't make the rules, I just enforce them."

"It's my way or the highway."

"It is what it is."

EMPLOYEE PERCEPTION

He thinks he's better than the rest of us, but he couldn't do my job.

He never says hello, thank you or good job. I'm not a person.

He's quick to place blame when things go wrong and take credit for success.

He doesn't respect me or my work.

I get the same response if I bust my butt as the guy who does nothing.

He's not interested in my professional or personal development.

He doesn't care about me, so why should I do what he wants?

Vanessa's Tips

Greet your team members every day. Get to know them. Talk to them about topics other than just work.

Model a positive, professional attitude each day. Speak positively at all times about customers, employees, departments and the company. This includes rules, policies and procedures. Be aware of your appearance and body language.

Understand what motivates your team and then do it! Say thank you in a way that is meaningful to *them*. Incentives and prizes don't work for everyone.

Ask questions. Understand their job and responsibilities. Help out when you can, but ask what they need first. Don't just jump in.

Ensure that everyone knows the team's goals, understands their role and the progress towards success. Tell them, post stats, update them regularly. Don't assume they know.

Communicate information personally sometimes. Keep employees updated on information that relates to them - company information, projects you are working on, upcoming events. Schedule regular meetings, then stick to the schedule.

Get out of your office! Be available to your employees. Spend time walking around your business daily. Observe and give feedback - positive feedback is best in public while corrective feedback should be given in private.

An open door may not be enough. Set "office hours" when you will be available to employees. This enables you to work, yet be prepared to be interrupted.
Invite people into your office for reasons other than discipline.

IAN VEESABLE:
YOU CAN BE TOO HANDS OFF

"INVISIBLE" MANAGER BELIEFS

- Hands off management means leaving them alone to do their work.
- I can't do their job, so I can't tell them what to do.
- They already know what to do, they don't need to be 'managed'.
- I will work behind the scenes to make their jobs easier.
- They don't want me hanging around looking over their shoulders.
- I'll step in if I think it looks like they need me.
- Not seeing a manager is a good thing.

EMPLOYEE'S PERCEPTION

He's not interested in what we do.

He doesn't care about employees.

We're not important enough to get a 'real' manager.

There is no one here to support me.

Things get done, but we're not even sure if it's the right things.

Nobody is held accountable. I work hard and Joe does nothing.

We don't feel like part of the team, so who cares?

Vanessa's Tips

Greet your team members every day. Talk to them about topics other than just work.

Get to know what they do in their jobs as well as their hobbies, interests, families, etc.

Ask questions. Understand their job and responsibilities. Help out when you can, but ask what they need first. Don't just jump in.

Ensure that everyone knows the team's goals, understands their role and the progress towards success.

Communicate information personally. Keep employees updated on information that relates to them - company information, projects you are working on, upcoming events.

Schedule regular meetings, then stick to the schedule.

Get out of your office! Be available to your employees. Spend time walking around your business daily. Observe and give feedback.

An open door may not be enough. Set "office hours" when you will be available to employees. This enables you to work, yet be prepared to be interrupted.

HEIDI JECKLE:
WORKING ON THE RIGHT FORMULA

"JECKLE AND HYDE" MANAGER BELIEFS

- I'm flexible.
- I empower my team.
- My boss expects me to know everything my team is doing.
- I'm supposed to have the answers and know everything.
- I'm not inconsistent. I respond to situations. I use a combination of management styles.

EMPLOYEE PERCEPTION

My manager doesn't know what he/she wants.

I won't do anything until they specifically tell me, so I don't have to do things twice.

This is so inefficient. I'm wasting my time.

I don't know what to expect from my manager.

I'm not sure if I'm doing a good job or not. The focus changes so quickly.

I'm reluctant to share my ideas and projects because I don't know how he/she will react.

I feel unproductive.

Vanessa's Tips

Make sure you clearly understand the team goals and expectations. Write them down to ensure that your daily tasks are related to your goals to avoid getting off track. Communicate information personally. Keep employees updated on information that relates to them - company information, projects you are working on, upcoming events

Ensure that everyone knows the team's goals, understands their role and the progress towards success. Provide feedback regularly. Let people know they are on the right track for success.

Get to know what they do in their jobs as well as their hobbies, interests, families, etc.
Ask questions. Understand their job and responsibilities. Help out when you can, but ask what they need first. Don't just jump in.

.

Schedule regular meetings, provide an agenda and then stick to it. This makes meetings more productive as everyone will be properly prepared. Occasional changes are expected. Constant changes encourage chaos.

Get out of your office! Listen to people. Be aware of business and employee issues, but avoid reacting to everyone. Keep focused.

DISCUSSION QUESTIONS

1. Describe some of the 'monstrous' behaviors you notice for this manager.

2. What beliefs does the manager hold that support their behaviors?

3. Which quadrant best describes this 'Monst-ager'?

4. What suggestions do you have for this manager moving forward with their team?